LIVING STONES

The all-age programme for Common Worship

Prayers of Intercession
Year B

SUSAN SAYERS

**kevin
mayhew**

First published in Great Britain in 1999 by Kevin Mayhew Ltd
Buxhall, Stowmarket, Suffolk IP14 3BW
Tel: +44 (0) 1449 737978 Fax: +44 (0) 1449 737834
E-mail: info@kevinmayhewltd.com

www.kevinmayhew.com

'Prayers of Intercession' is extracted from *Living Stones* – 'Complete Resource Book'.

9 8 7

ISBN 978 1 84003 395 3
Catalogue No. 1500294

The other titles in the *Living Stones* series are

Complete Resource Book	ISBN 978 1 84003 396 0	Catalogue No. 1500290
Pebbles	ISBN 978 1 84003 397 7	Catalogue No. 1500291
Rocks	ISBN 978 1 84003 398 4	Catalogue No. 1500292
Boulders	ISBN 978 1 84003 399 1	Catalogue No. 1500293

Cover design by Melody-Anne Lee
© Image copyright Artmann Witte. Used under licence from Shutterstock Inc.
Edited by Katherine Laidler
Typeset by Richard Weaver

Printed and bound in Great Britain

FOREWORD

A praying church is a living organism, powered by the love of God, and directed by his will. The aim of those leading intercessions in public worship is to provide a suitable climate for prayer, both for the faithful core of praying members, and also for those who drift in as visitors, sometimes willingly and sometimes rather grudgingly.

Since our God is in a far better position to know the needs of each muddle of people who arrive on any particular Sunday, it is obviously sensible to prepare for leading the intercessions by praying for those who will be there, asking our God to lead us with his agenda in mind, rather than taking immediate charge ourselves. Then we have to give him a chance to answer! You may find that a quiet walk enables you to do this, or a time wandering round the empty church, or time spent on some of the mechanical jobs at home while you still your heart and resist the temptation to badger God with good ideas.

I have provided ideas to reflect the day's readings, and as you read through them you may well find that these ideas will spark off other thoughts of your own. Do use them however you wish – exactly as they stand, adapted to suit specific needs, or simply as a starting point. They are a resource to help you, not a cage to keep your own ideas out.

During the service be alert to what is being said and how God is moving among you, so that you can pick up on these threads, if it seems appropriate, during the intercessions. And if you have young children present, give some thought to how they can also be praying at this time. They might be following a picture prayer trail, singing a quiet worship song, drawing some situation they are praying for, or looking through the intercession pictures provided in children's communion books, such as *Jesus is Here* (Kevin Mayhew, 1993).

I have heard it said that since God can hear the prayers, it doesn't really matter if the congregation can't. I don't agree. In public worship it can be very distracting to be straining to hear, or isolating if you can hear only a vague mumble. Do take the trouble to practise speaking clearly and fairly slowly in the church, so that everyone can comfortably take in what you are saying. Bear in mind that nerves usually make us speed up somewhat, so speak extra slowly to allow for this.

Finally, don't recite what you have written, but pray it. Pray it both through the intentions and through the silences. Leading the intercessions carries a great responsibility, but it is also a great privilege.

SUSAN SAYERS

CONTENTS

LENT

EASTER

ORDINARY TIME

First Sunday of Advent

Be alert and watchful; keep yourselves ready.

As we begin a new year in the life of the Church,
let us pray together to the God of our making.

Holy God, just as we are we come to you,
and ask for your kingdom to come in us
and in this place;
increase our faith and our love for you,
so that we may become the lights in darkness
that we are called to be.

Silence

O God, keep us awake to you:
and alive to your call.

Holy God, the signs in our world
of hate, distrust and greed
are shown to us clearly every day.
May we see with your eyes
the signs of hope and victory;
the opportunities for loving service,
for encouragement, reassurance and thanksgiving.

Silence

O God, keep us awake to you:
and alive to your call.

Holy God, bless the parenting and befriending
in all our relationships,
and increase our love for one another.
Give us the humility

to accept guidance and warnings, lovingly given,
and the courage to uphold one another in the faith.

Silence

O God, keep us awake to you:
and alive to your call.

Holy God, we bring to you in love
those who are weary with ongoing pain and weakness,
those who are frail with age and all who are vulnerable;
Pour your living strength into their lives
and protect them from all that is harmful.

Silence

O God, keep us awake to you:
and alive to your call.

Holy God, we pray for all
who have come to the end of their earthly life,
and for those whose lives feel empty without them.
Give comfort to the bereaved,
and everlasting peace to all who rest in your love.

Silence

O God, keep us awake to you:
and alive to your call.

Holy God, your faithful care
has brought us safely to this moment;
we thank you for your constant love, forgiveness,
strength and protection.

Merciful Father,
**accept these prayers
for the sake of your Son,
our Saviour Jesus Christ. Amen.**

SECOND SUNDAY OF ADVENT

John the Baptist prepares the way for the coming of the Messiah by helping the people to realign their lives.

As we gather expectantly in God's presence,
let us pray.

God of cleansing and liberating power,
give us the courage and perception
to see ourselves as we really are,
and repent of our sin;
may the whole Church be cleansed and renewed.

Silence

Come, O come, Emmanuel:
come and live in us.

God of wisdom and truth,
we pray for the world's leaders and all in authority,
that they may lead and govern wisely and honestly,
without corruption and for the common good.

Silence

Come, O come, Emmanuel:
come and live in us.

God of love and faithfulness,
may every family be surrounded and upheld
by your presence,
the conflicts healed and needs provided for,
and every act of kindness blessed.

Silence

Come, O come, Emmanuel:
come and live in us.

God of wholeness,
bring your reassurance and healing,
your hope and patience
to all who are suffering in any way;
bring freedom to all imprisoned by hate or guilt,
and a change of heart to all who need to forgive.

Silence

Come, O come, Emmanuel:
come and live in us.

God of unending life,
bring life in its fullness to us here,
and to those who have completed their time on earth.
May they know the freedom and joy of your heaven.

Silence

Come, O come, Emmanuel:
come and live in us.

God of warmth and brightness,
we praise you for all our many blessings,
and above all for coming to save us and set us free.

Merciful Father,
accept these prayers
for the sake of your Son,
our Saviour Jesus Christ. Amen.

Third Sunday of Advent

*In Jesus, God will be fulfilling the Messianic
prophecies about the promised Saviour.*

Let us pray now to the living God,
who always keeps his promises,
and who knows us so well.

Loving Father, keep the Church faithful
in telling the good news, comforting the desolate,
actively loving justice
and drawing many to freedom
through the joy of your forgiveness.

Silence

Keep us faithful:
to your calling.

As the Church, we pray for the world,
that there may be integrity in leadership;
mercy and justice for rich and poor,
strong and weak;
that there may be peace among nations
and respect for all.

Silence

Keep us faithful:
to your calling.

As the family of believers, we pray
for those around us now and their needs;
and for the families we represent, and their needs.

May the love of Christ be shown in what we do
and how we speak and how we spend.

Silence

Keep us faithful:
to your calling.

In compassion we call to mind
all who are locked in physical or emotional pain,
all who are weighed down with worry,
guilt or despair.
Restore and refresh them, comfort and free them.

Silence

Keep us faithful:
to your calling.

As resurrection people, we commend to your love
those who have died to this earthly life.
May they, and we in our turn, experience for ever
the joy of your eternity.

Silence

Keep us faithful:
to your calling.

As followers of the living Christ,
we praise you for the prophecies fulfilled,
the promises honoured and the victory over evil
gloriously accomplished in him
to fill our lives with hope.

Merciful Father,
accept these prayers
for the sake of your Son,
our Saviour Jesus Christ. Amen.

FOURTH SUNDAY OF ADVENT

God's promised kingdom, announced both to King David in ancient times and to Mary by the angel Gabriel, will go on for ever.

Gathered as the Church of God in this place,
let us pray together for the coming of the kingdom.

Lord of heaven, may the Church
be quiet enough to hear your voice,
humble enough to move your way,
and excited enough to spread the good news.

Silence

Living God:
let your kingdom come.

Lord of heaven, bless all who lead
with integrity and respect for others;
bless all in positions of authority
with humility and a sense of right;
may unjust practices be changed for good
and conflicts of great tension
be peacefully resolved.

Silence

Living God:
let your kingdom come.

Lord of heaven, make our homes
places of loving acceptance and developing faith;

teach us in all our friendships
to grow in generosity of spirit.

Silence

Living God:
let your kingdom come.

Lord of heaven, give patience and courage
to all who have to wait,
when the waiting is long and painful;
bring healing to all who are wounded,
whether physically or emotionally,
and give them assurance of your presence.

Silence

Living God:
let your kingdom come.

Lord of heaven, welcome into your eternity
those who have died to this life
and whose hope is in you.
Comfort those who mourn them
and reach into their pain with your love.

Silence

Living God:
let your kingdom come.

Lord of heaven, we thank you
for your faithful promise to us,
fulfilled in the coming of Jesus.
We welcome his kingship in our lives.

Merciful Father,
**accept these prayers
for the sake of your Son,
our Saviour Jesus Christ. Amen.**

CHRISTMAS DAY

*Jesus Christ, the world's Saviour,
is here with us, born as a human baby.*

As we gather to celebrate Christmas,
let us pray to the living God.

Lord God, thank you for our Church
and its people,
for our deacons, priests and bishops,
and all who pray.
Bless us all and strengthen us for your service
so we can touch the world with your love.

Silence

Holy God:
be born in us today.

Lord God, we thank you for our world
and all its beauty and blessing.
Teach us your ways, your love and your truth,
and let your kingdom grow and flourish.

Silence

Holy God:
be born in us today.

Lord God, we thank you for our families,
our neighbours and our friends,
for the happiness of human loving and sharing.
We pray for your blessing on all those we love,
whether present with us today or far away.

Silence

Holy God:
be born in us today.

Lord God, we thank you for health and strength,
and pray now for your help and healing
wherever people ache with pain and sorrow,
loneliness or fear.
Bless them in their need
and surround them with love.

Silence

Holy God:
be born in us today.

Lord God, we thank you for lives well lived,
and all who have guided us to you.
We pray for those who have died
and all for whom Christmas
sharpens the loss of loved ones.

Silence

Holy God:
be born in us today.

Lord God, we thank you for Christmas joy
and all the opportunities
to show our love for one another.
May our love, rooted in yours,
continue throughout the year.

Merciful Father,
**accept these prayers
for the sake of your Son,
our Saviour Jesus Christ. Amen.**

First Sunday
of Christmas

Just as the angels said, a Saviour has been born for us.

As we celebrate Jesus being born among us,
let us pray in the presence of God.

That the Church may truly be the Body of Christ,
in loving servanthood, humility and availability;
that as pastors and teachers,
prophets and evangelists,
givers, carers and listeners,
the whole people of God may make Christ known.

Silence

O come:
let us adore him.

That the world God loved into being
and placed in our care
may be valued and respected,
and its resources fairly shared.

Silence

O come:
let us adore him.

That every family may be blessed and guided
through all the troubles and chances of life,
supporting one another in love
and forgiving one another every day.

Silence

O come:
let us adore him.

That there may be food and shelter enough
for each person on this earth,
comfort and practical help for all in need
and peace of mind for the worriers.

Silence

O come:
let us adore him.

That the dying may be at peace with God,
and that those of our loved ones
who are separated from us through death
may know the joy of heaven.

Silence

O come:
let us adore him.

That our praises and thankfulness
may be bright as meadow flowers
springing up wherever we walk
through this daily gift of life you provide.

Merciful Father,
accept these prayers
for the sake of your Son,
our Saviour Jesus Christ. Amen.

SECOND SUNDAY OF CHRISTMAS

*The Word made flesh at Christmas was always
with God, always expressing his creative love.*

Let us pray to the God
who loves us enough to come and save us.

We pray for the areas of the Church
which are weak in faith,
despondent or complacent;
that we may be recharged
with the power of your love,
reawakened to the good news,
and revitalised with the breath of the Spirit.

Silence

Living Word of God:
be spoken in our lives.

We pray for all areas of misunderstanding
between peoples and nations,
between needs and offers of help;
make us more ready to listen than instruct,
more ready to encourage than crush.

Silence

Living Word of God:
be spoken in our lives.

We pray for family feuds and difficulties
to be resolved and learnt from;
for the words we speak

to express love and respect,
with true charity and forgiveness.

Silence

Living Word of God:
be spoken in our lives.

We pray for all who have difficulty
hearing and speaking,
reading and writing;
for the oppressed and persecuted
whose voices are silenced,
and for all who have yet to hear
the good news of God's love.

Silence

Living Word of God:
be spoken in our lives.

We pray for those who have died
and those who are dying now;
may your Word of life
encourage them on their journey
and bring them safely to your eternal kingdom.

Silence

Living Word of God:
be spoken in our lives.

We pray in thankfulness
for the joy of human communication
and the privilege of communing with the living God.

Merciful Father,
accept these prayers
for the sake of your Son,
our Saviour Jesus Christ. Amen.

THE EPIPHANY

Jesus, the promised Messiah,
is shown to the Gentile world.

Let us pray to the God who loves us
and knows the terrain we travel.

We thank God for all those who brought
the good news of Jesus to us,
and all who nourish our faith today.
We pray that the whole people of God
may work in unity and openness
for the coming of God's kingdom.

Silence

Lord God:
we offer you ourselves.

We thank God that salvation is for all people,
and pray for a just and accepting world
where none is rejected, despised
or treated with contempt.

Silence

Lord God:
we offer you ourselves.

We thank God for the privilege of parenting
and of living in communities;
we pray that our homes and churches
may be welcoming and generous-hearted.

Silence

Lord God:
we offer you ourselves.

We thank God for all who care
with such thoughtfulness and practical loving
for those who are vulnerable,
and especially for the very young.
We pray for healing and wholeness,
peace of mind, protection and hope.

Silence

Lord God:
we offer you ourselves.

We thank God for all who have reached
the end of their earthly journey in faith,
that they may be welcomed into your eternity.
May we use the time left to us here
as good stewards of God's gifts.

Silence

Lord God:
we offer you ourselves.

We thank God for including us
in the plan of salvation,
and pray that we may be made worthy
of our calling.

Merciful Father,
**accept these prayers
for the sake of your Son,
our Saviour Jesus Christ. Amen**

THE BAPTISM OF CHRIST FIRST SUNDAY OF EPIPHANY

*Through the Holy Spirit, Jesus is affirmed at his
Baptism as God's beloved Son, and we too are given
the Spirit of God which affirms us as God's
adopted daughters and sons.*

Let the Spirit of God in our hearts plead
for the Church and for the world.

Great God of all time and space,
fill the Church with such joy in believing
that all Christians overflow with love,
compassion, generosity and humility.
Let us walk your way and live your life.

Silence

May the Spirit of God:
fill us to overflowing.

Great God of power and justice,
fill the arenas of leadership and conflict
with sharpened consciences and with courage,
so that wise decisions are made,
needs met and wrongs righted.

Silence

May the Spirit of God:
fill us to overflowing.

Great God of gentleness and truth,
fill every home with new insight

and greater understanding.
Break down the divisive barriers
and build up our capacity to love.

Silence

May the Spirit of God:
fill us to overflowing.

Great God of attentive caring,
fill us with your practical compassion;
may all who suffer be heard,
comforted and cared for.
Heal both their situation and our hardness of heart.

Silence

May the Spirit of God:
fill us to overflowing.

Great God of unending being,
fill death with your life
and the dying with hope in you.
Prepare us all for life which lasts for ever.

Silence

May the Spirit of God:
fill us to overflowing.

Great God of all creation,
fill our mouths with praises
and our hearts with gratitude,
for all the glory that surrounds us.

Merciful Father,
accept these prayers
for the sake of your Son,
our Saviour Jesus Christ. Amen.

SECOND SUNDAY OF EPIPHANY

Jesus, the Christ,
unlocks the mysteries of God.

Let us pray to God,
who knows us better than we know ourselves,
and understands our world.

Lord, we know we are called
to be the Body of Christ;
make us worthy of that calling,
fervent in all our prayer and worship,
loving, faithful and honest in our lives,
so that the whole Church displays
what God is like.

Silence

Draw us closer:
closer to the heart of God.

We pray for the grace and wisdom
to care for this world we have been given as our home;
for perception in the difficult decisions,
and commitment to justice and peace.

Silence

Draw us closer:
closer to the heart of God.

We pray for the homes of this parish,
whose hopes and struggles, sorrows and fears
are already known to you.

May each household be blessed as we pray,
and may your love fill each life.

Silence

Draw us closer:
closer to the heart of God.

We pray for all who do not yet know you,
and all whose hearts are poisoned with hate
or weighed down with despair.
May your light scatter their darkness
and bring them hope and healing.

Silence

Draw us closer:
closer to the heart of God.

We pray for those who have died to this life
and are born into your heaven;
comfort those who miss their physical presence,
and bring us all to share in the fullness of your life.

Silence

Draw us closer:
closer to the heart of God.

We give you thanks for all that points us
towards the beauty of your love,
and draws us closer to you.

Merciful Father,
accept these prayers
for the sake of your Son,
our Saviour Jesus Christ. Amen.

THIRD SUNDAY OF EPIPHANY

*Signs of glory lead us to believe
in Jesus as Lord and Saviour.*

Drawn here by God,
let us bring to him our concerns
for the Church and the world.

We pray that the Church may be
a vibrant sign of God's life
in every generation and locality,
serving, listening and loving,
with the human face of ordinary people
lit with the brightness of God.

Silence

Direct us, Lord:
and we will follow.

We pray that the world's attention
may be refocused on what is of lasting value;
that in humility, all in authority
may hear the real needs,
honour them and act on them.

Silence

Direct us, Lord:
and we will follow.

We pray that all the households
and neighbourhoods represented here
may be alerted to the signs of glory around them

in the ordinary, daily miracles,
and come to welcome Jesus as Lord.

Silence

Direct us, Lord:
and we will follow.

We pray that all who are searching for God
may realise his closeness to them;
that wrong lives may be courageously righted,
and damaged lives and attitudes mended.

Silence

Direct us, Lord:
and we will follow.

We pray that the dying may turn to you
and be safely led through that last journey
to the peace and joy of eternal life.
We pray that we may all one day experience God's heaven.

Silence

Direct us, Lord:
and we will follow.

We pray that we may become increasingly aware
of God's amazing love for each of us,
until our hearts are overflowing
with thankfulness and praise.

Merciful Father,
**accept these prayers
for the sake of your Son,
our Saviour Jesus Christ. Amen.**

Fourth Sunday of Epiphany

*Jesus displays all the signs that mark
him out to be God's chosen One.*

As we gather in the presence
of the almighty, all-knowing God,
let us pray.

Holy God, great Spirit of all,
may the whole Church
honour and glorify your name
in daily lives, private prayer and public worship.

Silence

Holy God:
may your will be done.

May the whole world resound with your truth,
activate your compassion,
and be soaked in your peace.

Silence

Holy God:
may your will be done.

May all homes and households
make plenty of room for kindness and forgiveness;
clear the clutter of discontent,
and make us more thankful.

Silence

Holy God:
may your will be done.

May all who ache with sadness or physical pain
be comforted and cherished,
knowing your love for them.

Silence

Holy God:
may your will be done.

May the dying be surrounded with our prayers,
and those who have passed beyond death
remain safe for ever in your keeping.

Silence

Holy God:
may your will be done.

As we step into each new day
may our thanks and praise
give joy to the living God.

Merciful Father,
**accept these prayers
for the sake of your Son,
our Saviour Jesus Christ. Amen.**

PROPER 1

Sunday between 3 and 9 February inclusive
(if earlier than the Second Sunday before Lent)

The good news about God is far too good
to keep to ourselves.

We have gathered in the presence
of the one, holy God,
from whom all things take their being.
Let us pray to him now.

Wherever the sparkle of our vision has dulled,
set us glowing once again
at the very thought of you,
and restore our longing to draw closer to you
until our lives reflect your shining.

Silence

Who is the King of glory?
It is the Lord our God.

Wherever important and far-reaching decisions
need to be made,
wherever wrongs need righting
and justice needs to be restored,
breathe your wisdom and integrity
and let your kingdom come.

Silence

Who is the King of glory?
It is the Lord our God.

Wherever ongoing family conflicts need resolving,
wherever communication has broken down,

develop our capacity for unconditional loving,
and appreciation of every 'other'
as another child of your creating.

Silence

Who is the King of glory?
It is the Lord our God.

Wherever there is pain and suffering,
whether physical, emotional, mental or spiritual,
we pray for your fulsome healing,
and commit ourselves to be available
and ready to help.

Silence

Who is the King of glory?
It is the Lord our God.

As we call to mind those who have recently died
and those who will die today,
we pray for each of them,
that in their dying
they may find the greatest healing of all,
as they come into your holy presence for ever.

Silence

Who is the King of glory?
It is the Lord our God.

As we marvel afresh today
at your majesty and humility,
we thank you for the privilege of knowing you.

Merciful Father,
**accept these prayers
for the sake of your Son,
our Saviour Jesus Christ. Amen.**

Proper 2

Sunday between 10 and 16 February inclusive
(if earlier than the Second Sunday before Lent)

Jesus wants to heal us to wholeness,
and to him no one is untouchable.

Let us come to ask for the healing touch of our God
in the Church and in the world.

God of humility,
your desire to save us
made you willing to share our human brokenness;
as the Body of Christ, may the Church share
that willingness to be vulnerable
in order to serve in love.

Silence

Good physician:
heal us.

God of power,
your authority is gracious and merciful;
inspire all those with authority in our world
to be prompted by you,
so that they open the way
for your kingdom to be established.

Silence

Good physician:
heal us.

God of accepting love,
drive far from our homes and communities
all rejection and devaluing;

all justification for barriers;
and give us the courage to reach out in love.

Silence

Good physician:
heal us.

God of compassion,
shock us into seeing more clearly
the ache of those
whom society rejects and overlooks;
the wounds of the discarded
and socially embarrassing.
May we reach out where others turn away.

Silence

Good physician:
heal us.

God of eternity,
we remember those who, healed for ever,
live with you in the fullness of life.
We pray that we too may come, by your grace,
to share the life which has no ending.

Silence

Good physician:
heal us.

Lord, we thank you for the extent of your love
which has no limits
and no exceptions.

Merciful Father,
**accept these prayers
for the sake of your Son,
our Saviour Jesus Christ. Amen.**

PROPER 3

Sunday between 17 and 23 February inclusive
(if earlier than the Second Sunday before Lent)

The Son of Man has authority on earth to forgive sins.

In the sure knowledge that God cherishes us,
let us pray to him now.

Heavenly Father, so full of forgiveness and mercy,
fill your Church to the brim with such holiness
that our understanding of your ways
deepens daily,
and all our work and worship glorifies your name.

Silence

Holy God:
release in us your praise.

Heavenly Father, so wise and perceptive,
take us to the heart of all conflicts,
and give us the grace to share in the healing
between factions and nations,
guided by your Spirit.

Silence

Holy God:
release in us your praise.

Heavenly Father, so comforting and kind,
help us to notice the needs around us,
in our families, friends and colleagues,
and respond to them in love.

Silence

Holy God:
release in us your praise.

Heavenly Father, so mindful of our pain,
we bring to you our sisters and brothers
whose joints are stiff
and whose bodies cannot move freely;
thank you for their courage and example;
we pray that you will help their spirits to dance
and fill their hearts with joy.

Silence

Holy God:
release in us your praise.

Heavenly Father, so welcoming to all,
we commend to your everlasting keeping
those who have recently died,
and those who mourn their going.

Silence

Holy God:
release in us your praise.

Heavenly Father, so faithful in your promises,
we thank you for the eternal 'Yes' of Christ
which echoes on through lives and generations.

Merciful Father,
accept these prayers
for the sake of your Son,
our Saviour Jesus Christ. Amen.

SECOND SUNDAY BEFORE LENT

Christ is the image of the unseen God.

Our God made us and our universe,
and delights in us.
Prompted by the Spirit of God in us,
let us pray.

We pray for the godly wisdom
that is touched by the beauty of creation,
delights in the diversity of people,
and warms to the possibilities
of co-operative prayer and work
for the coming of the kingdom.

Silence

Wise and holy God:
we are your children.

We pray for the godly wisdom
that, in observing symptoms, discerns causes
and responds to the real needs;
that strives not to control but enable,
not to manipulate but empower.

Silence

Wise and holy God:
we are your children.

We pray for the godly wisdom
that gives others both space and support,
that encourages and guides,

that knows when to speak
and when to be silent.

Silence

Wise and holy God:
we are your children.

We pray for the godly wisdom
that recognises the poverty of the rich
and the wealth among the poor;
that questions assumptions of worth
and cherishes those whom the world discards.

Silence

Wise and holy God:
we are your children.

We pray for the godly wisdom
that sees time in the context of eternity,
and death as the gateway to heaven.

Silence

Wise and holy God:
we are your children.

We pray for the godly wisdom
that lives simply and thankfully,
rejoicing in all that God is and does.

Merciful Father,
accept these prayers
for the sake of your Son,
our Saviour Jesus Christ. Amen.

Sunday before Lent

God's glory shows.

Let us pray to the God of glory,
revealed to us in his Son, Jesus.

Father, lengthen and deepen our attention span
as we, your people, listen to your beloved Son,
so that we do not fail to hear his will for us
or share his longing for the world to be saved.

Silence

Let us worship the Lord:
in the beauty of holiness.

Father, with such humility you entered the world
to save it through love's giving;
increase our desire to enter into
one another's suffering and hardship,
to share the world's resources fairly
with one another,
and recognise all humanity as brothers and sisters.

Silence

Let us worship the Lord:
in the beauty of holiness.

Father, let us not take one another for granted,
but wake each morning ready to notice the Christ
in each person we see and speak to;
and reverence your hidden presence
in all creation.

Silence

Let us worship the Lord:
in the beauty of holiness.

Father, in our prayer we stand alongside
all who are too weak to pray, or too confused;
may all who are suffering
sense your love and comfort,
and be given strength to persevere,
and peace of mind and spirit.

Silence

Let us worship the Lord:
in the beauty of holiness.

Father, we commend to your eternal presence
those who have recently died,
that they may rest in peace and rise in glory.

Silence

Let us worship the Lord:
in the beauty of holiness.

Father, thank you for providing always
the encouragement and inspiration we need
for the work you would have us do;
give us the grace to trust your will for us
and walk forward boldly in your company.

Merciful Father,
accept these prayers
for the sake of your Son,
our Saviour Jesus Christ. Amen.

FIRST SUNDAY OF LENT

After his Baptism Jesus is led by the Spirit into the wilderness before returning to proclaim God's kingdom.

As we begin this season of Lent,
let us move off into the desert
to communicate with our God.

Lord God, we come with all our muddled priorities,
and conflicting agendas,
to be made whole as the Body of Christ;
to renounce evil so as to be equipped
to announce the kingdom of peace.

Silence

With our God:
all things are possible.

Lord God, we come with the world's clamour
ringing in our ears,
with comfort zones beckoning us,
but the pain of injustice refusing to be shut out.
We come for the world's healing,
and for an end to all lying and deceit.

Silence

With our God:
all things are possible.

Lord God, we come with the demands
of home, family, work and expectations
warring in us for space and attention.

We come on behalf of those
too busy or too exhausted to pray;
that our daily lives may be washed in your peace,
ordered in holiness and lit up with your joy.

Silence

With our God:
all things are possible.

Lord God, we come with the needs and sorrows,
pain and suffering of our brothers and sisters
all over the world, who are aching –
physically, emotionally or spiritually;
we come to ask your comfort and healing love.

Silence

With our God:
all things are possible.

Lord God, we come to realign our lives
in the context of your eternity,
and to commend to your love our own loved ones
who have passed through earthly death
to the life which has no ending.

Silence

With our God:
all things are possible.

Lord God, we come with thankfulness
for the gift of life, and for the call to holiness.
Give us the grace to respond to your calling.

Merciful Father,
accept these prayers
for the sake of your Son,
our Saviour Jesus Christ. Amen.

SECOND SUNDAY OF LENT

A commitment of faith has far-reaching implications.

Let us pray to our God in faith,
knowing that he understands what is best for us.

Heavenly Father, increase our faith,
that everyone in your Church
may be more ready to trust you
and move forward with you
wherever you lead us.

Silence

You speak what is true:
and the truth can set us free.

Heavenly Father, give to all leaders
and their advisers
the courage to be honest,
the will to be just,
the greatness to be humble
and the openness to learn.

Silence

You speak what is true:
and the truth can set us free.

Heavenly Father, at the door of each home
place your welcome;
in the rooms of each home, your love;

in the eyes of each person, your truth;
and in all our companionship, your own.

Silence

You speak what is true:
and the truth can set us free.

Heavenly Father, give comfort and healing
to those who are ill,
peace to the anxious,
and reassurance to the afraid;
may we know your love for us
through both the good and the agonising times.

Silence

You speak what is true:
and the truth can set us free.

Heavenly Father, may the dying be prepared
to meet you,
and the souls of those who have died in faith
live for ever in the joy of your presence.

Silence

You speak what is true:
and the truth can set us free.

Heavenly Father, give us thankful hearts
to bless your name in sadness and in joy,
knowing that you are always there beside us.

Merciful Father,
**accept these prayers
for the sake of your Son,
our Saviour Jesus Christ. Amen.**

THIRD SUNDAY
OF LENT

*God's wisdom may shock us. Jesus, obedient to
God's Law and fulfilling it, dies a death which,
according to the Law, makes him cursed.*

As God has called us,
so we have come to pray.

We pray for the Church, the Body of Christ,
with all its collected gifts and weaknesses;
give us the grace to recognise
that in your Spirit we are one,
and curb in us all tendency to division.

Silence

May we hear you, Lord:
and want to obey.

We pray for the world
in all its beauty and richness;
give us the desire
to share our planet's food and resources,
to care for its people's well-being,
and to foster peace and justice for all.

Silence

May we hear you, Lord:
and want to obey.

We pray for those we love –
those we see each day and those we miss;

help us to cherish one another
as we live the loving way of your commands.

Silence

May we hear you, Lord:
and want to obey.

We pray for all victims of selfish or violent acts,
and for those whose lives are trapped in sin.
We pray for all whose bodies and minds
have difficulty functioning.
Make us more sensitive to their needs.

Silence

May we hear you, Lord:
and want to obey.

We pray for those who have died
and for those who miss their physical presence.
Have mercy on them;
may they, and we in our turn,
rest in the peace of your enfolding.

Silence

May we hear you, Lord:
and want to obey.

We give you thanks
for the loving example of Jesus,
who was obedient even to death
and strengthens us in all goodness.

Merciful Father,
**accept these prayers
for the sake of your Son,
our Saviour Jesus Christ. Amen.**

Fourth Sunday of Lent
Mothering Sunday

*God provides comfort in all
our troubles and sufferings.*

As we gather together
in the presence of our parent God,
let us pray.

Loving Father, we pray
for all who are persecuted for their faith,
and for whom following you brings danger.
We pray for those who are new to faith
and those who no longer walk with you.
We thank you for the example of those
whose faith shines out in their lives.

Silence

We are all your children:
help us grow in love.

Loving Father, we pray
for those who are forced to leave their homes,
their families or their countries.
We pray for those who, through war and famine,
must watch their children die.
We pray for your peace and comfort.

Silence

We are all your children:
help us grow in love.

Loving Father, we pray
for all the mothering that goes on in this community

and for those who crave tenderness
and are weary of the struggle to be strong.

Silence

We are all your children:
help us grow in love.

Loving Father, we pray
for all new parents and their babies,
and all giving birth today.
We pray for all who are vulnerable,
that they may be protected from harm.

Silence

We are all your children:
help us grow in love.

Loving Father, there are those here
whose mothers have died,
and are still remembered with great affection.
We pray for those mothers and grandmothers now,
rejoicing in all they gave,
and commending them to your protection for ever.

Silence

We are all your children:
help us grow in love.

Loving Father, we give you thanks
for the comfort you provide in all our troubles,
and for the richness of all our relationships.

Merciful Father,
accept these prayers
for the sake of your Son,
our Saviour Jesus Christ. Amen.

FIFTH SUNDAY OF LENT

*Through Christ's death, full life would come
to people of all nations and generations.*

Let us pray to the God who loves us
and understands our needs.

God of mercy, we pray for all Church leaders,
teachers and pastors,
and all who are being called
into particular ministries, both lay and ordained.
We pray especially for any who are wrestling
with the demands of such a calling,
that they may be given courage
to offer themselves in your service.

Silence

Let your name be glorified:
let your will be done.

All-seeing God, watch over the nations of the world
in all their plans and actions, conflicts and disasters;
guard the children, guide the leaders
and give us all your peace.

Silence

Let your name be glorified:
let your will be done.

God of love, be present in every heart and home,
to cherish, to challenge,
to reassure and to comfort us.

Silence

Let your name be glorified:
let your will be done.

God of wholeness, we bring to your love
those who are weighed down with suffering,
or imprisoned by their fears.
Ease their burdens and give them the strength
to bear what cannot be avoided.

Silence

Let your name be glorified:
let your will be done.

God of life, we bring to you those
whose earthly lives have ended,
that in your mercy they may have everlasting peace.

Silence

Let your name be glorified:
let your will be done.

Gracious God, you are always
so much more ready to give than we to receive;
open our hearts and minds
to live the costly way of love.

Merciful Father,
accept these prayers
for the sake of your Son,
our Saviour Jesus Christ. Amen.

PALM SUNDAY

As the Messiah, Jesus enters Jerusalem,
knowing that he rides towards rejection
and death in order to save his people.

As we face up to the costly loving
shown by our God,
let us approach him in humility
and pray to him now.

O God, give us in your Church undivided hearts
to love you and one another, and go on loving,
through insult and praise,
through acceptance and rejection,
in the sure knowledge that you are Lord.

Silence

Make us strong:
to do your will in all things.

O God, may the kingdoms of this world
soak up the values of your kingdom;
may their leaders and their peoples
uphold what is right and just,
and establish a social order
which is rooted in Godly love.

Silence

Make us strong:
to do your will in all things.

O God, in all the heartaches and joys
of human relationships,
may we be governed by selfless love,

faithful and forgiving like you,
without limit.

Silence

Make us strong:
to do your will in all things.

O God, draw alongside all who suffer
that they may know the comfort of your presence
and the healing power of your forgiving love.

Silence

Make us strong:
to do your will in all things.

O God, we pray for all
who are making that last journey of death,
that they may be surrounded with your peace
and rest in your love for ever.

Silence

Make us strong:
to do your will in all things.

O God, we give you thanks
that the Messiah has come to save your people.

Merciful Father,
accept these prayers
for the sake of your Son,
our Saviour Jesus Christ. Amen.

EASTER DAY

*Jesus is alive; Love has won the
victory over sin and death.*

As we celebrate the risen Christ,
let us pray to the God of life,
in whom we live.

That the Church of God
may be bursting with new life,
filled with the love
that takes even death in its stride;
that new and mature Christians together,
all in their various ministries,
may work in God's strength
for the coming kingdom.

Silence

You are our God:
who does all things well.

That the inhabitants of our planet
may recognise God's glory all around,
co-operate in the sharing of his gifts,
and cultivate the habit of caring love.

Silence

You are our God:
who does all things well.

That God will bless our homes and families,
our places of work and leisure,

with new life and the hope of new possibilities
touching the ordinary with beauty and joy.

Silence

You are our God:
who does all things well.

That all who feel trapped or imprisoned –
physically, mentally or spiritually –
may feel the stones rolled away
and new light pouring into their lives.

Silence

You are our God:
who does all things well.

That those who have died to this earthly life
may find the fullness of God's eternity,
flooded with the light of his love.

Silence

You are our God:
who does all things well.

That we may live each moment thankfully,
assured of God's company and mercy.

Merciful Father,
**accept these prayers
for the sake of your Son,
our Saviour Jesus Christ. Amen.**

SECOND SUNDAY OF EASTER

*Our faith in the risen Christ
is bound to affect the way we live.*

Knowing that the risen Christ is here among us,
let us pray in his name
for the Church and for the world.

Father, we pray for your blessing
on every group of Christians worshipping today
all over the world;
and we pray for all who doubt your truth.
We pray that our hearts may be set ablaze
with love,
and that we may walk as children of light.

Silence

My Lord and my God!
My Lord and my God!

Father, we pray for all the areas of your world
which are torn apart by hatred and violence,
famine, disease, or religious differences;
we pray for an end to war
and a deeper commitment to peace.

Silence

My Lord and my God!
My Lord and my God!

Father, we pray for those who face family rejection
if they become Christians,
and for all families divided by beliefs

or persecuted for their faith.
We pray for the children of our church
that they may grow up strong in the faith
with good role models to guide them.

Silence

My Lord and my God!
My Lord and my God!

Father, we pray for those who wake up
to the prospect of another day filled with pain;
for those who long for someone
to spend time with them, enjoying their company;
and we pray for sight that notices needs.

Silence

My Lord and my God!
My Lord and my God!

Father, we pray for those who mourn,
and we pray for those they love and miss,
commending all who have died
to the everlasting arms of the God of love,
in whom there is life in all its fullness.

Silence

My Lord and my God!
My Lord and my God!

Father, with joy in our hearts we thank you
for the new life opened up to us
through Jesus, our Redeemer.

Merciful Father,
accept these prayers
for the sake of your Son,
our Saviour Jesus Christ. Amen.

THIRD SUNDAY OF EASTER

*Having redeemed us by his death, Jesus can offer us
the forgiveness of our sin, which sets us free to live.*

May God be glorified now,
as we commit ourselves to the work of prayer,
interceding for those in all kinds of need.

In our worship,
and our openness to the Spirit of life,
in the Church's longing and outreach,
in the priests, the people,
in all seekers and honest doubters,

in all this:
may God be glorified.

Silence

In the welfare programmes
and peace-making missions,
in the struggle to uphold justice,
in the aid given to the hungry and homeless,

in all this:
may God be glorified.

Silence

In the loving and costly commitment
of mothers and fathers, brothers and sisters,
daughters and sons,
in the determination to forgive and forgive,
in all the lives shared and cherished,

in all this:
may God be glorified.

Silence

In the work of nursing, comforting and healing,
in the daily patient struggle
with pain and weakness,
and in the practical, good-humoured caring,

in all this:
may God be glorified.

Silence

In the twilight years and the facing of death,
in lives well lived and now breaking into eternity,

in all this:
may God be glorified.

Silence

In the freedom offered through forgiveness,
in the joy of Resurrection life,
in the hope of eternity,

in all this:
may God be glorified.

Silence

Merciful Father,
accept these prayers
for the sake of your Son,
our Saviour Jesus Christ. Amen.

FOURTH SUNDAY OF EASTER

*'I am the Good Shepherd
and I lay down my life for the sheep.'*

The Lord is our Shepherd;
knowing his care for us, let us pray.

For all who shepherd others
as bishops and pastors,
and for all in their care;
for Christians threatened and under attack;
and all whose ministry feels demanding.
For a greater affection and care,
one for another, in the Church.

Silence

The Lord is our Good Shepherd:
there is nothing we shall lack.

We pray for all in positions of leadership
and influence in our world,
that they may use that power for good;
for an increase in our concern
for one another's well-being, across all barriers,
and for all who are working to build community.

Silence

The Lord is our Good Shepherd:
there is nothing we shall lack.

We pray for those who are wandering, lost and aimless,
with no idea that any Good Shepherd exists;

for those who die unaware that they are precious
and valued by the God who loved them into being.

Silence

The Lord is our Good Shepherd:
there is nothing we shall lack.

We pray for those who have died
to this earthly life,
that the Good Shepherd,
who understands what it is to die,
may bring them safely home.

Silence

The Lord is our Good Shepherd:
there is nothing we shall lack.

We pray in thankfulness
for your shepherding of us,
and own you as our Good Shepherd
in whom we are kept safe for ever.

Merciful Father,
accept these prayers
for the sake of your Son,
our Saviour Jesus Christ. Amen.

FIFTH SUNDAY
OF EASTER

*To produce fruit we need to be
joined on to the true vine.*

Let us pray to the Lord God Almighty,
in whom we live and move and have our being.

Father, we want to produce good fruit in abundance;
nurture us as branches of the true vine,
train and prune us where necessary,
and may our spiritual harvest make rich wine,
wine of your kingdom.

Silence

Your kingdom, let it come!
Your will, let it be done!

Father, clearly we see around our world
the tragic and expensive consequences
of branches cut off from the true vine.
We pray for a seeking after your truth
and a desire to act rightly and justly
in all areas of human society.

Silence

Your kingdom, let it come!
Your will, let it be done!

Father, we pray for those to whom we are linked
by family, friendships or work;
especially we pray for those
separated from their loved ones or their home.

Silence

Your kingdom, let it come!
Your will, let it be done!

Father, we long for healing and wholeness
in all who suffer
and in all dysfunctional communities;
guide us to understand
how we might be part of the healing.

Silence

Your kingdom, let it come!
Your will, let it be done!

Father, we know that death
cannot separate us from your love;
in that knowledge we commend to your keeping
those who have died and all who miss them.

Silence

Your kingdom, let it come!
Your will, let it be done!

Father, we thank you that we can live
in the joyful freedom of your love,
as we dedicate ourselves to serving others.

Merciful Father,
**accept these prayers
for the sake of your Son,
our Saviour Jesus Christ. Amen.**

SIXTH SUNDAY OF EASTER

We are to love one another as Jesus loves us.

Knowing God's love and affection for us,
let us pray to him now.

Father, wherever there is friction and conflict
in the Church,
and communities are divided and weakened;
give us a greater longing for your healing
and a deeper commitment to forgiving love.

Silence

Help us, Lord:
to love one another.

Father, wherever tangled political situations
seem impossible to solve,
wherever conflicting interests threaten peace;
wherever the ears of the powerful
remain insulated against the cries of the oppressed;
give us ears to hear your guidance.

Silence

Help us, Lord:
to love one another.

Father, wherever families are dysfunctional
or children are in danger;
wherever the daily living conditions

are damaging to health and self-respect;
let your kingdom come.

Silence

Help us, Lord:
to love one another.

Father, wherever the ill and injured
need comfort and assistance;
wherever the elderly and housebound
sit each day for hours alone;
may we bring your love and help.

Silence

Help us, Lord:
to love one another.

Father, wherever people are travelling
that last journey of death,
may they be surrounded by your love
and welcomed into your heaven,
and may those who mourn be comforted.

Silence

Help us, Lord:
to love one another.

Father, wherever the beauty of creation
reflects your love,
may our hearts be lifted to you
in thanks and praise.

Merciful Father,
accept these prayers
for the sake of your Son,
our Saviour Jesus Christ. Amen.

ASCENSION DAY

Having bought back our freedom with the giving of his life, Jesus enters into the full glory to which he is entitled.

Rejoicing that Jesus has ascended into the heavens,
let us pray in confidence to God our Father.

We pray in thankfulness
for those who introduced us to Jesus
and who help us along our spiritual journey.
We pray for one another in this church
and for all Christians, young and old,
throughout the world.

Silence

Let the kingdom come:
let your kingdom come.

We pray with longing
for the world to be governed
in accordance with your law of love;
that all your creation may be reverenced
and treated with respect.

Silence

Let the kingdom come:
let your kingdom come.

We pray with concern
for all the homes, schools and places of work
in this community;
rejoicing in all that is of you,

and asking your healing forgiveness
wherever there is discord or bitterness.

Silence

Let the kingdom come:
let your kingdom come.

We pray with hope
for the healing and restoration to wholeness
of all who are ill or troubled,
damaged or depressed.

Silence

Let the kingdom come:
let your kingdom come.

We pray with confidence
for those who have come to the end
of their earthly lives,
that they may be given merciful judgement
and welcomed into the glory of heaven.

Silence

Let the kingdom come:
let your kingdom come.

We pray with joy
as we celebrate Jesus entering the glory
he so richly deserves, and look expectantly
towards his second coming.

Merciful Father,
**accept these prayers
for the sake of your Son,
our Saviour Jesus Christ. Amen.**

Seventh Sunday of Easter

Although now hidden from our sight,
Jesus lives for ever, and in him we can live
the Resurrection life even while we are on earth.

Let us pray together to our heavenly Father,
knowing his love for us.

Father, we want to live your way
and do your will,
offer you true worship,
and serve one another in love.
Empower your Church to do this, we pray;
live in us; transform us.

Silence

Lord, we wait on you:
fill us, Holy Spirit of God.

Father, we want our states and kingdoms
to display your love and truth, justice and mercy.
We want to break down walls of prejudice
and build bridges of reconciliation and trust.
Empower your world, we pray;
live in us; transform us.

Silence

Lord, we wait on you:
fill us, Holy Spirit of God.

Father, we want our children
to be safely and lovingly nurtured,
our elderly valued,

our homes to be places of welcome and warmth;
empower your people, we pray:
live in us; transform us.

Silence

Lord, we wait on you:
fill us, Holy Spirit of God.

Father, we want your healing
for those whose lives are aching and weary;
your comfort and reassurance
for all who are imprisoned by fears and hate;
empower these lives, we pray;
live in us; transform us.

Silence

Lord, we wait on you:
fill us, Holy Spirit of God.

Father, we want to commit our loved ones,
who have died, into your safe keeping for ever.
Prepare us all, Father, to live with you in heaven.

Silence

Lord, we wait on you:
fill us, Holy Spirit of God.

Father, we want to worship and praise you
with our voices and our lives;
shape us to your purpose, and use us.

Merciful Father,
accept these prayers
for the sake of your Son,
our Saviour Jesus Christ. Amen.

PENTECOST

The Holy Spirit of God is poured out in power on the expectant disciples, just as Jesus promised.

In the power of the Holy Spirit,
let us pray.

For a fresh in-breathing of life and power
in each church community,
which breaks down our barriers
and sets us on fire with God's love.

Silence

Come, Holy Spirit:
Holy Spirit, come!

For the grace to see this world
and its needs and problems
through the eyes of love, hope,
justice and mercy;
for the grace to abandon prejudice
and build bridges of reconciliation.

Silence

Come, Holy Spirit:
Holy Spirit, come!

For the Spirit of loving kindness
to fill our homes, schools and places of work;
for family rifts to be healed
and long-standing conflicts resolved.

Silence

Come, Holy Spirit:
Holy Spirit, come!

For the restoration of those who are sick
to wholeness and well-being;
for courage and patience in all suffering,
and for good to be distilled
from every painful, destructive experience.

Silence

Come, Holy Spirit:
Holy Spirit, come!

For God's merciful judgement
on those who have died,
and the opportunity for us all
to prepare carefully for meeting God
face to face.

Silence

Come, Holy Spirit:
Holy Spirit, come!

For a deeper knowledge and love
of the God who knows and loves us completely.

Merciful Father,
accept these prayers
for the sake of your Son,
our Saviour Jesus Christ. Amen.

TRINITY SUNDAY

*The mysterious and holy nature of the one true
God is beyond our understanding, but it is
both communal harmony and individual
personality, Father, Son and Holy Spirit.*

Let us pray to the Father
through the Son
and in the power of the Holy Spirit.

Lord God, may the Church reflect
your community and unity;
may there be Godly harmony, shared ministry,
mutual support and encouragement in the faith.

Silence

May your will be done:
on earth as it is in heaven.

Lord God, may the world's leaders
seek not personal power but the public good;
may conflicts be faced honestly
and needs recognised and met;
may all our communities be built up
on what is good, true, just and right.

Silence

May your will be done:
on earth as it is in heaven.

Lord God, may there be love and respect
for one another in every household;

may there be mutual support
and thoughtfulness, consideration and trust.

Silence

May your will be done:
on earth as it is in heaven.

Lord God, may the hearts' cries for help be heard;
the tears collected and the fears quieted;
may suffering be eased and guilt erased
through your healing love.

Silence

May your will be done:
on earth as it is in heaven.

Lord God, may the dead rise
to new and eternal life,
freed from their aching and restored for ever.

Silence

May your will be done:
on earth as it is in heaven.

Lord God, we pour out to you
our praise and wonder
at the hidden mysterious holiness
of your Being, so full of glory and love!

Merciful Father,
**accept these prayers
for the sake of your Son,
our Saviour Jesus Christ. Amen.**

PROPER 4

Sunday between 29 May and 4 June inclusive
(if after Trinity Sunday)

Jesus has the words of eternal life – he sheds
light on a right attitude to the Law.

Through Jesus
we are shown God's compassion and mercy;
let us pray for that love in our lives,
in the Church and in the world.

Let compassion and mercy
be the hallmarks of our church life
and all its activities;
let us be noticeable by their shining
in our behaviour and our conversations;
disrupt any rules which block them out.

Silence

Lord of love:
let only your will be done.

Let compassion and mercy
take root in every institution, policy and structure;
let them challenge accepted wrongs
and disturb complacency.

Silence

Lord of love:
let only your will be done.

Let compassion and mercy
guard every doorway and fill every room;

let them colour each encounter
and drive every decision.

Silence

Lord of love:
let only your will be done.

Let compassion and mercy
transform our attitudes
to all whose illness or frailty
makes them marginalised, ignored or despised.
Let there be healing of all damaged self-perception,
and restoration of jarred human dignity.

Silence

Lord of love:
let only your will be done.

Let compassion and mercy
accompany the dying
and welcome them into eternity.

Silence

Lord of love:
let only your will be done.

Let compassion and mercy
blossom in all of us,
as we live out our thankfulness
to the God of love,
for all his goodness to us.

Merciful Father,
accept these prayers
for the sake of your Son,
our Saviour Jesus Christ. Amen.

PROPER 5

Sunday between 5 and 11 June inclusive
(if after Trinity Sunday)

*Anyone who does God's will is considered
a close family member of Jesus.*

As members of God's family,
let us pray together to our heavenly Father.

That as family members of the Church of God
we may show his likeness by doing his will;
that those visiting our churches
may find there God's beauty and truth,
open-hearted loving and a unity of purpose.

Silence

Father:
let your will be done.

That as members of the human race
we may work together, share resources,
respect and learn from one another.
That leaders may inspire collective good,
and those with vision be valued and heard.

Silence

Father:
let your will be done.

That we may give both support and space
to those we love and nurture;
that those of our own families
who do not yet know God

may come to understand the depth
of his love for them.

Silence

Father:
let your will be done.

That all who come to Jesus in need
may find in him forgiveness, healing
and wholeness of body, mind and spirit,
strength to cope with their difficulties
and a constant inner renewing.

Silence

Father:
let your will be done.

That as those coming to death
roll up the tents of their earthly existence,
they may be welcomed into the eternal home
prepared for them by their loving God.

Silence

Father:
let your will be done.

That as we marvel at the generosity
of God's love, and his acceptance of us,
we may grow closer to his likeness
each day we live.

Merciful Father,
**accept these prayers
for the sake of your Son,
our Saviour Jesus Christ. Amen.**

PROPER 6

*Sunday between 12 and 18 June inclusive
(if after Trinity Sunday)*

*From small beginnings, and by God's power,
the kingdom of heaven grows.*

Let us pray to the God of heaven and earth
for the growth of the kingdom.

May the kingdom grow
in clusters of Christians all over the world;
may it grow as hearts are warmed
by encounter with the living God;
nourished by word and sacrament,
private prayer and public worship.

Silence

Lord of heaven:
let the kingdom grow!

May the kingdom grow
in states, empires and monarchies,
in the crowded streets of cities
and in the scattered rural communities;
in all decision-making and all spending.

Silence

Lord of heaven:
let the kingdom grow!

May the kingdom grow
in every human shelter and home,
every place of work and education,

in each conversation and
in our mutual care of one another.

Silence

Lord of heaven:
let the kingdom grow!

May the kingdom grow
to bring peace and healing
wherever there is pain or sadness;
to bring reassurance, comfort, courage and hope.

Silence

Lord of heaven:
let the kingdom grow!

In the knowledge that we must all face judgement,
we pray for those who have died,
thanking God for his loving mercy,
and entrusting our loved ones
to God's safe keeping.

Silence

Lord of heaven:
let the kingdom grow!

As we thank God for all his blessings to us
we offer him the rest of our lives.

Merciful Father,
accept these prayers
for the sake of your Son,
our Saviour Jesus Christ. Amen.

PROPER 7

Sunday between 19 and 25 June inclusive
(if after Trinity Sunday)

What kind of person is this?
Even the wind and waves obey him.

As residents of God's universe,
let us pray now to our loving Creator.

Lord of all truth and goodness,
we pray for those in positions of authority
in the Church all over the world
and in each gathered community;
that in all the storms
we may be enabled to hear God's calming voice
and deepen our trust in him.

Silence

Calm our fears:
and teach us your peace.

Lord of great power and majesty,
we pray for those with political and military power,
and all whose decisions affect many lives.
Speak truth into motives, honour into actions
and your vision of peace into every conflict.

Silence

Calm our fears:
and teach us your peace.

Heavenly Father, we pray for all single people,
couples, communal groups and families,
as they weather their storms and learn from them;

lavish on all who have the care of others
the capacity to bring peace and calm fears.

Silence

Calm our fears:
and teach us your peace.

Lord of all healing, we pray for those
whose minds and hearts are in turmoil,
whose lives lurch from crisis to crisis;
for those who find their lives shattered
by illness or injury;
for peace in those threatening storms
and a settling of all anxiety.

Silence

Calm our fears:
and teach us your peace.

Lord of eternity, we thank you
for your reassurance of life beyond physical death;
we pray for those who are dying alone,
unnoticed or unprepared;
we commend those who have died
to God's merciful forgiveness and eternal tranquillity.

Silence

Calm our fears:
and teach us your peace.

Lord of creation,
we are full of wonder at the story of your universe,
spoken into existence and sustained with such love.

Merciful Father,
accept these prayers
for the sake of your Son,
our Saviour Jesus Christ. Amen.

PROPER 8

Sunday between 26 June and 2 July inclusive

God's power can reach even into death and draw out life.

As God has called us by name
out into full, abundant life,
let us lay before him now our concerns
for the Church and for the world.

Father, chip away from your Church
all the built-up layers
of complacency or despondency,
of over-comfortable familiarity
or under-active expectation,
until we see again
with the freshness and wonder of deepened faith.

Silence

Lord, we believe:
help our unbelief.

Father, we call to mind
societies and systems of our world.
Question our assumptions
and challenge our destructive choices;
break away the unnoticed scales of prejudice
which blind us,
so that our world may become
increasingly under your reign of justice,
righteousness and love.

Silence

Lord, we believe:
help our unbelief.

Father, replace our pride with humility
until we learn from young children
the lessons of wonder and trust.
Keep the childlike as a living flame
in all of us, whatever our age,
and enable us to rediscover your glory all around us.

Silence

Lord, we believe:
help our unbelief.

Father, as the sick were brought to Jesus
by their loved ones,
so we bring to you now all those
whom we long to be healed.
May they hear your voice and sense your touch.

Silence

Lord, we believe:
help our unbelief.

Father, earth-bound we grieve
at the loss of loved ones through death;
yet we also rejoice in you calling them out
into the fullness of everlasting life.

Silence

Lord, we believe:
help our unbelief.

Father, we thank you for the amazing truth
that you always reach out to us in compassion,
and always have time for us.

Merciful Father,
**accept these prayers
for the sake of your Son,
our Saviour Jesus Christ. Amen.**

PROPER 9

Sunday between 3 and 9 July inclusive

*If we are not ready to listen to the truth,
we will not hear it.*

God has drawn us down many different routes
to this shared worship today.
Let us still our bodies
and alert our minds and hearts in his presence.

Heavenly Father, we are only the Body of Christ
because your Spirit binds us together with your life.
Give us real concern and love for one another,
supportive and encouraging,
without malice or bickering,
so that we can be sent out
strong in our weakness and littleness.

Silence

Give us your grace:
to hear your word with joy.

Heavenly Father, all the kingdoms and states
are answerable to your authority,
and much evil is allowed to flourish
through the silence of good people;
give us all the courage to speak out your truth,
whether it is popular or not.

Silence

Give us your grace:
to hear your word with joy.

Heavenly Father, be in all our listening
at home, on the phone, at school and at work;

may we give our full attention to you
and to one another,
happy to grow wiser through each conversation.

Silence

Give us your grace:
to hear your word with joy.

Heavenly Father, we pray for those
whose pain screams silently and incessantly;
for those who have no one to confide in,
no one to listen.
We pray for your love to enfold them,
your peace to calm them
and your healing to transform them.

Silence

Give us your grace:
to hear your word with joy.

Heavenly Father, prepare us all during this life
for the life to come;
we commend to your keeping all those
who have recently made their journey through death.

Silence

Give us your grace:
to hear your word with joy.

Heavenly Father, we thank you
for making your ways known to us
and guiding us into your truth.

Merciful Father,
accept these prayers
for the sake of your Son,
our Saviour Jesus Christ. Amen.

PROPER 10

Sunday between 10 and 16 July inclusive

*Those who speak out God's will are bound
to be vulnerable to rejection and abuse.*

In humility and love
let us draw near to our God
and pray to him now.

Lord God, we pray that our lives
may be upright and holy;
that our church communities may shine
with goodness and love, humility and truth;
we pray for all leaning lives to be straightened up
through your merciful forgiveness.

Silence

Holy God, scatter all darkness:
and bathe our world in your light.

Lord God, we pray that many
may be empowered to recognise evil
and fight against it;
to discern your warnings and speak them out;
to notice the sparks of love and goodness
and celebrate them.

Silence

Holy God, scatter all darkness:
and bathe our world in your light.

Lord God, we pray that our households
and neighbourhoods,

our places of work and leisure,
may be arenas of praise and thankfulness,
not only in the comfort zones
but particularly through the disturbed
and difficult times.

Silence

Holy God, scatter all darkness:
and bathe our world in your light.

Lord God, we pray for those in prison;
for those leading cruel and violent lives;
for all victims of oppression or abuse;
for all who suffer mental anguish or physical pain.

Silence

Holy God, scatter all darkness:
and bathe our world in your light.

Lord God, we pray for those who have died,
that they, and we in our turn, may be given
merciful judgement through Jesus our Saviour,
and brought into the unquenchable light of heaven.

Silence

Holy God, scatter all darkness:
and bathe our world in your light.

Lord God, we pray for more thankful hearts
to bless you, because the gifts we receive from you
are so much more than we deserve.

Merciful Father,
accept these prayers
for the sake of your Son,
our Saviour Jesus Christ. Amen.

PROPER 11

Sunday between 17 and 23 July inclusive

*Like a good shepherd, Jesus sees the needs
of his people and always responds with love.*

Knowing God's love and concern for us all,
let us settle ourselves in his presence
and pray to him now.

Recognising our brokenness and disunity
as your Church,
we pray for your leading
to draw us closer to one another
as we draw closer to you;
we pray for all our Christian brothers and sisters
in this neighbourhood,
and for all who are searching for meaning in their lives.

Silence

The Lord is my shepherd:
there is nothing I shall want.

With the noise of global conflicts
and human deprivation thundering in our ears,
with the questions and doubts clamouring,
we pray for your shepherding of our humanness
and your leading in the secret places of the heart.

Silence

The Lord is my shepherd:
there is nothing I shall want.

With the statistics of family life
challenging our values,

and with the pressures to conform to norms
in conflict with God's will,
we pray for your sound and centred wisdom
in all our daily living and life choices.

Silence

The Lord is my shepherd:
there is nothing I shall want.

With the stressed and overburdened,
the overworked and the unemployed,
we pray for balanced lives;
for physical, mental and spiritual health;
for patience in times of trouble,
and direction in times of confusion.

Silence

The Lord is my shepherd:
there is nothing I shall want.

As we remember with love and gratitude
the lives of those who have died in faith,
we commend them to your eternal rest
and unchanging affection.

Silence

The Lord is my shepherd:
there is nothing I shall want.

With the crowds of Galilee
our hearts are lifted with joy at your presence among us,
for we know that you have the words of eternal life.

Merciful Father,
accept these prayers
for the sake of your Son,
our Saviour Jesus Christ. Amen.

PROPER 12

Sunday between 24 and 30 July inclusive

*Out of God's riches, a great crowd is fed and satisfied
from a small offering of food.*

Knowing that our loving God
supplies all our needs,
let us pray to him now
on behalf of the Church and the world.

Father, we offer this time and the love of our hearts
as we pray for the Church with all its varied ministries;
for the youngest to the oldest baptised members;
for those of mellow faith
and those who struggle with doubts.

Silence

Loving Father:
give us today our daily bread.

Father, we offer our commitment
to pray the news each day
and share the pain we read about,
longing for your peace and your justice
in a world tense with aggression
and distorted with selfishness.

Silence

Loving Father:
give us today our daily bread.

Father, we offer our homes and our relationships
for you to work in and transform;
we offer you our meetings and conflicts

and all differences of opinion
for you to use to your glory.

Silence

Loving Father:
give us today our daily bread.

Father, we offer you our solidarity
with all who suffer or are heavily burdened;
hear us as we pray
for their comfort and refreshment,
wholeness and restoration,
but above all for the consciousness
of your presence in their pain,
and your love for them.

Silence

Loving Father:
give us today our daily bread.

Father, we offer our thanks for lives well lived
and faithful souls entering by the gate
of physical death to eternal life with you.
Prepare us all to meet you face to face.

Silence

Loving Father:
give us today our daily bread.

Father, we give you our lives
as well as our words of praise,
so that each moment from now on
becomes an offering of love.

Merciful Father,
**accept these prayers
for the sake of your Son,
our Saviour Jesus Christ. Amen.**

PROPER 13

Sunday between 31 July and 6 August inclusive

*Jesus is the Bread of Life who satisfies our hunger
and sustains us on our journey to heaven.*

Let us pray to the God who loves us,
knows our needs, and provides for us.

As the travelling people of God,
we pray for a deepening hunger
for the things of God
and a loosening of our grip
on all the wants and expectations
which prevent us from moving forward God's way.

Silence

Feed us, Father:
with the Bread of Life.

As brothers and sisters with the whole of creation,
we pray for respect and reverence among people
regardless of wealth or status;
for responsible sharing of resources
and consideration for the natural world
of our fragile and beautiful planet.

Silence

Feed us, Father:
with the Bread of Life.

As we prepare and eat our food each day,
we pray for those who grow and manufacture it,
distribute and sell it, shop for it and cook it,
and for those with whom we share food.

Build us up with your spiritual feeding
which sustains us for ever.

Silence

Feed us, Father:
with the Bread of Life.

As we ask for daily bread,
we pray for those who are physically starving,
for all who hunger emotionally
or try to survive on spiritual junk food;
for those who mistrust God's feeding.

Silence

Feed us, Father:
with the Bread of Life.

As we remember with love
those who have journeyed through physical death,
we pray that, nourished by the Bread of Life,
they may travel on eagles' wings
into the brightness of eternal life.

Silence

Feed us, Father:
with the Bread of Life.

As we grow increasingly aware
of our spiritual hunger,
we give thanks for the wonder of God's feeding,
throughout our days.

Merciful Father,
accept these prayers
for the sake of your Son,
our Saviour Jesus Christ. Amen.

PROPER 14

Sunday between 7 and 13 August inclusive

*Just as bread is the visible form of life-giving
nourishment, so Jesus is the visible form
of God's life-giving love.*

Let us pray to our God
as we worship him in Spirit and in truth.

Heavenly Father, we pray for all
who are commissioned and called
to work as leaders and prophets in your Church.
We pray for greater discernment of your presence
and your will in our Christian communities,
and a clearing away of all that obscures our vision.

Silence

Open our eyes:
to see your glory.

Heavenly Father, we pray against the cynicism
and complacency that deaden wonder.
In the ordinary things of life
may we detect your love and wisdom;
through the everyday events
may we encounter you, walking alongside us.

Silence

Open our eyes:
to see your glory.

Heavenly Father, we pray for breadwinners
and sandwich makers, and all food growers;

for your presence in kitchens, dining rooms,
canteens, restaurants and bars;
wherever people gather to eat together,
may they find you there with them.

Silence

Open our eyes:
to see your glory.

Heavenly Father, we pray for those
whose emotional damage makes trusting and receiving
seem threatening and dangerous.
We pray for peace of mind for the anxious,
and hope for all who are close to despair.

Silence

Open our eyes:
to see your glory.

Heavenly Father, we pray for those
who have reached the boundary of death,
that in faith they may journey through it
and out into the unconfined space and joy of heaven.

Silence

Open our eyes:
to see your glory.

Heavenly Father, we rejoice
that the ordinary things of this world
are saturated with your extraordinary love.

Merciful Father,
accept these prayers
for the sake of your Son,
our Saviour Jesus Christ. Amen.

PROPER 15

Sunday between 14 and 20 August inclusive

*God's wisdom may appear foolishness without
the God-given grace to understand.*

As we gather, conscious of our need of wisdom,
let us pray to our wise and loving God.

Father, in all the decision-making,
problems and challenges of our church,
we ask your counsel and encouragement;
in all our worship and outreach,
we invite you to lead us.

Silence

Wise and loving God:
quieten us to hear your voice.

Father, in all the clashes of needs and wants,
the half-forgotten hurts that drive aggression
the half-remembered grievances,
barbed with revenge,
in all the world's raging and protesting,
sink your spirit of peace and reconciliation.

Silence

Wise and loving God:
quieten us to hear your voice.

Father, in the daily batch of misunderstandings,
conflicting loyalties, negotiations and compromise,
walk among us in our homes and places of work,
whispering sanity and mutual respect.

Silence

Wise and loving God:
quieten us to hear your voice.

Father, in those engulfed by pain
or enslaved by addiction,
bring hope and healing;
bless all those whose minds think simply
and rely on others for basic care.

Silence

Wise and loving God:
quieten us to hear your voice.

Father, gather into your keeping for ever
all who have left this life in your friendship;
we pray too for those approaching death,
that they may know your love
surrounding them across time and eternity.

Silence

Wise and loving God:
quieten us to hear your voice.

Father, in all our wondering and wandering,
we thank you for your patience with us
and your understanding of our journey.

Merciful Father,
accept these prayers
for the sake of your Son,
our Saviour Jesus Christ. Amen.

PROPER 16

Sunday between 21 and 27 August inclusive

'To whom else could we go?
You alone have the words of eternal life.'

We have chosen to serve the Lord.
Let us pray to him now.

We pray for those whose faith
is being challenged or undermined
by inner doubts or outside influences.
We pray for those who build up our faith
and all who strive to proclaim the Gospel
in language that people understand.

Silence

Holy God, we believe:
help our unbelief.

We pray for our torn and fragmented world,
wrestling to equate the deep yearning for peace
with the instinctive urge for gratification and power;
that many may have the courage to walk God's way.

Silence

Holy God, we believe:
help our unbelief.

We pray for our loved ones;
for those who lift our hearts
and those who turn our hair grey.
We pray for those we instinctively warm to
and those with whom

there are frequent misunderstandings.
We thank God for our opportunities of forgiveness.

Silence

Holy God, we believe:
help our unbelief.

We pray for all who are marginalised,
scorned or rejected;
for those isolated through illness or imprisonment;
for those who feel that no one understands.
Surround them all with such love
that they may know they are precious to you.

Silence

Holy God, we believe:
help our unbelief.

We pray for those approaching death,
that through our prayers they may know themselves
accompanied with love on that journey.
We pray for those who have died,
that they may come to know the full joy of heaven.

Silence

Holy God, we believe:
help our unbelief.

We thank you, Holy God,
for making yourself known to us,
both in daily living
and sacramentally in the breaking of bread.

Merciful Father,
accept these prayers
for the sake of your Son,
our Saviour Jesus Christ. Amen.

PROPER 17

Sunday between 28 August and 3 September inclusive

*We need to be careful never to replace the timeless
commands of God with man-made traditions.*

Our God is the source of all holiness;
with the needs of the Church and the world
close to our hearts,
let us pray to the only one
who can renew and redeem.

Father, we are all too aware of our temptation
to place our trust in rules and traditions,
and we long for you to release in the Church
such a desire to serve the living God
that nothing is allowed to get in the way of that.

Silence

Into your hands, O Lord:
we commit the future.

Father, we recognise in ourselves
the universal dangerous wants and cravings
which are cultivated because they make money.
Give us universally such a loathing of evil
that there is international co-operation
and individual responsibility in fighting it
and building one another up in love.

Silence

Into your hands, O Lord:
we commit the future.

Father, may our homes, schools and churches
reflect and engender the Godly values

of mutual care, respect and responsibility,
of integrity and forgiveness.

Silence

Into your hands, O Lord:
we commit the future.

Father, we stand alongside all who are hurting
in body, mind or spirit;
all who need courage, support or practical help.
Make us willing to become
part of your answer to our prayers for them.

Silence

Into your hands, O Lord:
we commit the future.

Father, as Lord of both time and eternity,
we commit to your keeping
those who have died to this life;
that, freed from all pain, and forgiven,
they may live in the peace and joy of heaven.

Silence

Into your hands, O Lord:
we commit the future.

Father, write your Law of love on our hearts
and send us glowing with thankfulness
through the week ahead.

Merciful Father,
**accept these prayers
for the sake of your Son,
our Saviour Jesus Christ. Amen.**

PROPER 18

Sunday between 4 and 10 September inclusive

Jesus comes fulfilling the hope of healing to wholeness;
he shows that mercy has triumphed over judgement.

Let us pray to our loving and merciful God.

Lord, we thank you for the richness and diversity
of each unique identity.
We pray for the separate members
of this Body of Christ, and our corporate nature,
that we may be filled at every level
with the living breath of God.

Silence

Father of mercy:
let your kingdom come.

We thank you for the beauty and variety
of our landscapes and cultures, all over the world;
for starscapes and the wideness of space.
Teach us to cherish and respect
this universe we inhabit
and all those who look or sound different
from ourselves.

Silence

Father of mercy:
let your kingdom come.

We thank you for the hope
each newborn child brings;
for the gentle gifts of laughter and friendship,

thoughtfulness and sympathy.
We pray that our eyes may see all others
with God's affection.

Silence

Father of mercy:
let your kingdom come.

We thank you for the patient endurance
of so many who suffer so much;
for them all we pray your wholeness
and refreshing,
your upholding and healing.

Silence

Father of mercy:
let your kingdom come.

We thank you for the promise of mercy
triumphing over judgement,
and commend to your love for ever
our own loved ones who have died.

Silence

Father of mercy:
let your kingdom come.

We thank you for all our blessings
and pray that we may take none of them
for granted,
but commit ourselves to live out
our thanks each day.

Merciful Father,
accept these prayers
for the sake of your Son,
our Saviour Jesus Christ. Amen.

PROPER 19

Sunday between 11 and 17 September inclusive

*Loving obedience to God is shown by Jesus
to be a quality rich in courage and wisdom,
a quality to be highly respected.*

As sons and daughters of our heavenly Father,
responding to his call,
let us bring to him our needs and concerns.

That we may all learn to think God's way
and desire to do his will above everything else;
that we may be ready to suffer if necessary,
and put ourselves out, and do that cheerfully,
considering it a privilege.

Silence

In the spirit of obedience:
we ask your guidance.

That the craving to be most powerful
may be transformed into a yearning
for mutual respect and harmony;
that wealth may not shout louder than right,
and the whisper of truth may be heard
above the clamour of expediency.

Silence

In the spirit of obedience:
we ask your guidance.

That within our homes and places of work
we may practise self-discipline in all that we say,
and in the way it is said,

using our mouths to speak wisely and positively
with love in both hearts and voices.

Silence

In the spirit of obedience:
we ask your guidance.

That those whose bodies or spirits
are heavy with suffering
may be given courage and hope,
ease from the pain, and healing to wholeness.
That we may know how best to help them.

Silence

In the spirit of obedience:
we ask your guidance.

That those who have died in faith
may rise to eternal life,
and that we may so live on earth
that we are all prepared
for meeting you face to face in heaven.

Silence

In the spirit of obedience:
we ask your guidance.

That, as we rejoice in the perfect love
and obedience of Jesus,
we may find his life transforming ours.

Merciful Father,
**accept these prayers
for the sake of your Son,
our Saviour Jesus Christ. Amen.**

PROPER 20

Sunday between 18 and 24 September inclusive

*The truly great in God's eyes are those who are
prepared to be last of all and servant of all.*

Let us pray to the God of glory
in whom we live and move and have our being.

We pray that the Church may hold true
to the teaching of Jesus, without being persuaded
that worldly values of status and ambition
are suitable or acceptable in Christ's followers.
We pray for a spirit of humility
to deflate all pomposity and arrogance.

Silence

Yours, Lord, is the kingdom:
yours the power and yours the glory.

We pray that all in positions of power,
authority and influence in our world
may recognise their calling to servanthood
and never lose their identity
with the needs and longings of those they serve.

Silence

Yours, Lord, is the kingdom:
yours the power and yours the glory.

We pray that all communities
may look after one another,
supporting the vulnerable, encouraging the timid,

providing practical help for all who need it,
and nurturing the young in a climate of trust.

Silence

Yours, Lord, is the kingdom:
yours the power and yours the glory.

We pray that none may be considered expendable,
or beyond our cherishing;
we pray for all who have lost heart,
through pain, suffering or sin,
that God's redeeming power may work its wonders
in the very darkest situations.

Silence

Yours, Lord, is the kingdom:
yours the power and yours the glory.

We pray that all who have wearily
struggled to death
may know the joy of burdens laid down,
and new, lasting life transforming them
through the eternal love of God.

Silence

Yours, Lord, is the kingdom:
yours the power and yours the glory.

We pray that we may find new joy
in giving and serving freely, without thanks,
rejoicing in the privilege of following Jesus.

Merciful Father,
accept these prayers
for the sake of your Son,
our Saviour Jesus Christ. Amen.

PROPER 21

Sunday between 25 September and 1 October inclusive

*Don't let your body lead you into sin and risk
exchanging eternal life for eternal punishment.*

Conscious of our need for God's power
in our lives, our Church and our world,
let us pray to him now.

Father, as you have called us to be salt,
give us the courage to reject sin and evil
in our own lives
and in the corporate life of the Church.
May our churches be powerhouses of your Spirit,
training and upholding us
as we live your life in the world.

Silence

Your Law, O Lord, is perfect:
it revives the soul.

Father, we pray for a greater awareness
of what damages souls and encourages evil,
and for widespread commitment
to addressing the dangers.
We pray for all who earn their living
through selling what destroys lives.

Silence

Your Law, O Lord, is perfect:
it revives the soul.

Father, we pray for the young,
and the vulnerable in every community,

for all in positions of trust,
for child-minders, playgroups and schools,
for children's clubs and the uniformed organisations,
for loving nurture and protection from all evil.

Silence

Your Law, O Lord, is perfect:
it revives the soul.

Father, we pray for all long-term carers
and those they look after,
for all who are having to learn dependence gracefully,
and those who are imprisoned by their guilt.
Work your healing love in them all,
reassuring them of your presence.

Silence

Your Law, O Lord, is perfect:
it revives the soul.

Father, we pray that no one may be lost eternally,
that all may turn from their sin and trust your mercy;
that physical death may be but the gate to heaven.
We commend to your love
those who have recently died.

Silence

Your Law, O Lord, is perfect:
it revives the soul.

Father, we offer you our thanks and praise
for sins forgiven, and the joy
of walking through life in your company.

Merciful Father,
**accept these prayers
for the sake of your Son,
our Saviour Jesus Christ. Amen.**

PROPER 22

*Human beings are made responsible for the care of creation
but are subject to God in all aspects of their lives.*

Let us come before God our Maker,
making our prayers to him,
through Jesus and in the power of the Holy Spirit.

We pray that the Church may be alive
to God's beckoning,
quick to obey his will
and always ready to act in his loving service
for the good of the world.

Silence

Lord of heaven:
let your will be done.

We pray that all leaders and heads of state
may take wise advice and act responsibly
for the well-being of all.
We pray for God's guidance
in the way we manage and care for this planet,
its resources, riches and inhabitants.

Silence

Lord of heaven:
let your will be done.

We pray for all marriages,
for those seeking marriage partners
and those whose marriages are under strain.

We pray for all in close relationships,
that there may be mutual love and respect.

Silence

Lord of heaven:
let your will be done.

We pray for all who are suffering
through illness, accident or deliberate cruelty;
for refugees and all who are abused;
that through the caring of human hands
they may experience the caring hands of God.

Silence

Lord of heaven:
let your will be done.

We pray for all who have died violently
or suddenly, or with no one to miss them.
May all who have died in faith
be judged with mercy
and welcomed into eternal life.

Silence

Lord of heaven:
let your will be done.

We pour out our thanks and praise
for the gift of life
and the gift of one another.
May we treat each other with renewed reverence.

Merciful Father,
accept these prayers
for the sake of your Son,
our Saviour Jesus Christ. Amen.

Proper 23

Sunday between 9 and 15 October inclusive

The word of God is living and active, piercing right to the heart; only with God is it possible to be saved.

Let us lay down our own agendas
and seek the face of God,
and his will for the Church and for the world.

We pray for all who are seeking God,
and for the nurturing process in this parish.
We pray for opportunities to share God's love
and draw others to meet him.

Silence

Your will be done:
on earth as in heaven.

We pray for all who are fighting against evil
for goodness, truth and justice,
both those who make the world news
and those whose battles are known only to God.
We pray for our country and its leaders,
that this nation may seek God.

Silence

Your will be done:
on earth as in heaven.

We pray that wealth and comfort may not divert us
from searching out the heart of God;
that we may hear God's challenging
and gladly respond to him;

that our homes and communities
may sparkle with God's glory.

Silence

Your will be done:
on earth as in heaven.

We pray for the disillusioned and depressed
and all who have lost their way in life;
we pray for those corrupted by evil,
trained in hatred and twisted by bitterness.
We pray for the transforming of these lives.

Silence

Your will be done:
on earth as in heaven.

We pray for those whose earthly life
has come to an end,
and for those who mourn their going.
May the dead rest in the peace and joy of heaven
through the mercy of God.

Silence

Your will be done:
on earth as in heaven.

With thankful hearts we recall the times
when God has rescued and forgiven us,
leading us deeper into his friendship.

Merciful Father,
**accept these prayers
for the sake of your Son,
our Saviour Jesus Christ. Amen.**

PROPER 24

Sunday between 16 and 22 October inclusive

*Even the Son of Man himself came not to be served
but to serve, and to give his life as a ransom for many.*

In humility and love, let us pray together
to the God of our making and redeeming.

That all Christians may fulfil their vocation
to be servants, caring for the needs of others,
obedient to their Lord in all things
and supportive of one another
in worship, prayer and deepening faith.

Silence

Into your hands, O Lord:
we commit our prayers.

That those who govern and advise
may seek out God's will
and the good of all
in each crisis, dilemma and debate.

Silence

Into your hands, O Lord:
we commit our prayers.

That we may develop the habit
of rejoicing in the opportunities to serve,
and to put ourselves out for others,
laying down our craving for praise
and importance.

Silence

Into your hands, O Lord:
we commit our prayers.

That those who suffer in mind, body and spirit
may sense the Christ close beside them,
knowing his healing and resting in his love.

Silence

Into your hands, O Lord:
we commit our prayers.

That those who have died in faith
may be welcomed into the light of heaven,
and that all who are walking in sin today
may turn away from evil, and live.

Silence

Into your hands, O Lord:
we commit our prayers.

We thank you, Lord God,
for your long-suffering patience with us,
and the affectionate forgiveness
which lifts us to our feet whenever we stumble.

Merciful Father,
accept these prayers
for the sake of your Son,
our Saviour Jesus Christ. Amen.

PROPER 25

Sunday between 23 and 29 October inclusive

*In Jesus, God gathers his scattered people
and opens their eyes to see.*

As children of our heavenly Father,
trusting in his will and capacity to care for us all,
let us pray.

We pray for all pastoral care in the Church,
for the ministries of listening and counselling;
the sharing of grief; the freeing from guilt.
We pray for the grace to accompany
others to Christ's healing love.

Silence

What do you want God to do for you?
Lord, we want to see.

We pray for the healing of the nations;
for a recognition of our need of God
and a turning away from all that is evil.
We pray for all in authority and worldly power,
that they may be guided along right paths.

Silence

What do you want God to do for you?
Lord, we want to see.

We pray for an increase in love for one another,
that we may be better at recognising needs
and responding to them;
that we may give more time to those we love.

Silence

What do you want God to do for you?
Lord, we want to see.

We pray for those who are blind
or partially sighted,
and those who are spiritually or emotionally blind.
We pray for the opening of eyes to see God's way
and faith to trust him through good and ill.

Silence

What do you want God to do for you?
Lord, we want to see.

We pray for those whose eyes
have shut to this world,
that they may open to the brightness
and joy of heaven.

Silence

What do you want God to do for you?
Lord, we want to see.

We thank you, heavenly Father,
for drawing us to you
and stretching out your arms to us in welcome.

Merciful Father,
**accept these prayers
for the sake of your Son,
our Saviour Jesus Christ. Amen.**

ALL SAINTS' DAY

Sunday between 30 October and 5 November inclusive

Great is the rejoicing in heaven among the saints
of God as they worship their Lord in glory.

Let us still our bodies
and open our hearts and minds to pray.

We pray for all the saints on earth,
all those walking as friends of Jesus
through the light and shadows of life,
in grassy meadows and scaling bare rock;
that we may all persevere with joy,
supporting one another along the way.

Silence

Not our will, Lord:
but yours be done.

We pray for all the kingdoms and nations of the earth,
for their leaders and their people,
their policies and needs,
that under God's overarching love
they may learn his ways and his will.

Silence

Not our will, Lord:
but yours be done.

We pray for those we love and care for
and those who love and pray for us,
for the wisdom to learn
from all we experience in this life,

so that we are not damaged,
but rather grow from the difficult times.

Silence

Not our will, Lord:
but yours be done.

We pray for those who are suffering
and those too weak to pray;
for all who are searching for life's meaning
and those who find it hard to believe
they are loved and cherished by the living God.

Silence

Not our will, Lord:
but yours be done.

We pray for those who have died in faith,
giving thanks for the shining lives of the saints,
and asking that with them
we may come to share
in the endless joy of heaven.

Silence

Not our will, Lord:
but yours be done.

With thankfulness we celebrate
the transforming love of God,
which can take us as we are
and make us into what God can already see
we could become.

Merciful Father,
**accept these prayers
for the sake of your Son,
our Saviour Jesus Christ. Amen.**

Fourth Sunday before Advent

Sunday between 30 October and 5 November inclusive*

* For use if the Feast of All Saints was celebrated on 1 November
and alternative propers are needed

*To love the living God with heart, soul and strength,
and to love our neighbour as ourselves means far
more than any sacrificial offerings.*

As God's people, gathered in his presence,
let us pray.

For all who preach and teach the Gospel
in word and sacrament
throughout the worldwide Church.
For those who lead prayer groups
and Bible studies,
and all who gossip their faith to others.

Silence

O Lord our God:
in you we trust.

For all who are tortured or persecuted
for what they believe;
for the voiceless and powerless,
for the powerful and coercive.

Silence

O Lord our God:
in you we trust.

For greater respect for one another
as children of God's making;

for God's presence in each conversation,
discussion and debate,
each concern and celebration.

Silence

O Lord our God:
in you we trust.

For healing and wholeness,
mending and comforting,
calming and refreshing,
wherever lives and bodies ache.

Silence

O Lord our God:
in you we trust.

For everlasting peace in the arms of God
for those who have come to the end
of their life on earth
and comfort for all who grieve.

Silence

O Lord our God:
in you we trust.

We give thanks for God's constant love
which upholds our being
and cradles our living in his hand.

Merciful Father,
accept these prayers
for the sake of your Son,
our Saviour Jesus Christ. Amen.

THIRD SUNDAY BEFORE ADVENT

Sunday between 6 and 12 November inclusive

*When we are called we need to respond with obedience
so that many may be brought to repentance.*

Let us pray to the God who has called us to be here,
bringing to him the cares of our Church and our world.

We pray for deeper faith among Christians,
and a readiness to respond to God's calling.
For those being called to particular ministries
and those called to change their way of living,
we pray for courage, and the grace to obey.

Silence

Unfailing love is yours, Lord:
you are our rock of refuge.

We pray for all who feel pressurised
to conform to wrong values
in order to be accepted;
for a commitment to fight evil
and cultivate good in our world.

Silence

Unfailing love is yours, Lord:
you are our rock of refuge.

We pray for the households of this parish
and God's indwelling there;

for guidance in the everyday decisions
and the times of crisis.

Silence

Unfailing love is yours, Lord:
you are our rock of refuge.

We pray for the weak, the vulnerable,
the weary and the desolated;
for those entrenched in sin
and endangering others.

Silence

Unfailing love is yours, Lord:
you are our rock of refuge.

We pray for those who have died
in God's friendship,
and give thanks for their lives.
May they be called into the light of heaven.

Silence

Unfailing love is yours, Lord:
you are our rock of refuge.

In thankfulness we pray
for those who called us to repentance
and offered us the hope of new life in Christ.

Merciful Father,
accept these prayers
for the sake of your Son,
our Saviour Jesus Christ. Amen.

SECOND SUNDAY BEFORE ADVENT

Sunday between 13 and 19 November inclusive

We are to be on our guard; great anguish will accompany the last days, but all that is good and loving, wise and true will be saved and celebrated for ever.

As God's love has drawn us,
let us pray.

That the Church may grow and flourish,
protected from evil within and without;
that in worship and ministry
God's love may be brought into places of darkness
and offer many the light of hope.

Silence

Lord our God:
show us the path of life.

That our shrinking world
may bring about co-operation
and a fresh appreciation of one another's cultures;
that we may encourage one another
in goodness, peace and love.

Silence

Lord our God:
show us the path of life.

That we may take time
to cherish our loved ones in the present moment,
and value the blessings we receive each day.

Silence

Lord our God:
show us the path of life.

That God's healing touch
may bring wholeness and peace
to those who suffer,
and hope to those who are close to despair.

Silence

Lord our God:
show us the path of life.

That God's love may surround those
travelling through death
and bring them safely to heaven.

Silence

Lord our God:
show us the path of life.

We praise and bless you, Lord,
for Christ's saving death
and the promise of everlasting life.

Merciful Father,
accept these prayers
for the sake of your Son,
our Saviour Jesus Christ. Amen.

CHRIST THE KING

Sunday between 20 and 26 November inclusive

*Jesus Christ is the everlasting King whose
kingdom is not of this world, but grows in
the hearts of his people and lasts for ever.*

As children of the kingdom,
let us make our prayers to the eternal God,
who loves us.

We pray for your kingdom to come
in the worldwide communities
of those who believe in Jesus Christ –
may our lives enthrone him.

Silence

Spirit of the living God:
may your kingdom come.

We pray for your kingdom to come
in the nations of our world
and in their leadership;
for God's values to take root and grow;
for each person to be respected
as a beloved child of God.

Silence

Spirit of the living God:
may your kingdom come.

We pray for your kingdom to come
in our homes and families,

our neighbourhoods and places of work,
in all thinking, all speaking and all action.

Silence

Spirit of the living God:
may your kingdom come.

We pray for your kingdom to come
in all hospitals and surgeries,
and in every place of pain and sadness.

Silence

Spirit of the living God:
may your kingdom come.

We pray for your kingdom to come
in the final stages of earthly life,
in the journey through death,
and in the awakening to eternal life.

Silence

Spirit of the living God:
may your kingdom come.

We thank you for making us,
and redeeming us,
opening wide to us the gates of heaven.

Merciful Father,
accept these prayers
for the sake of your Son,
our Saviour Jesus Christ. Amen.